OCCASIONAL
PAPER

T0302553

Recasting NATO's Strategic Concept

Possible Directions for the United States

Christopher S. Chivvis

Prepared for the United States Air Force

RAND PROJECT AIR FORCE

The research described in this report was sponsored by the United States Air Force under Contract FA7014-06-C-0001. Further information may be obtained from the Strategic Planning Division, Directorate of Plans, Hq USAF.

Library of Congress Cataloging-in-Publication Data is available for this publication.

ISBN 978-0-8330-4873-8

Published 2009 by the RAND Corporation
1776 Main Street, P.O. Box 2138, Santa Monica, CA 90407-2138
1200 South Hayes Street, Arlington, VA 22202-5050
4570 Fifth Avenue, Suite 600, Pittsburgh, PA 15213-2665
RAND URL: http://www.rand.org/
To order RAND documents or to obtain additional information, contact
Distribution Services: Telephone: (310) 451-7002;
Fax: (310) 451-6915; Email: order@rand.org

Preface

In spring 2009, the North Atlantic Treaty Organization (NATO) began to revise its strategic concept. The revision is an opportunity to build consensus and steer the alliance in a direction that will help keep it relevant in the future. Recognizing that the document that emerges will express a consensus view, this paper examines five possible directions that the strategic concept might take. The purpose is to offer an intellectual framework for discussions, based on concrete options.

These directions were developed through a process of internal RAND Corporation discussion and debate and reflect RAND expertise on NATO and on the major strategic challenges the alliance will face in the next decade. The directions developed were then assessed against certain key political and military criteria. The aim is to offer a range of options along with an assessment of the feasibility and potential implications of each.

Funding for this work was provided as a concept-formulation activity of the Strategy and Doctrine Program of RAND Project AIR FORCE. Support was also provided through RAND's program of self-initiated research. Support for such research is provided, in part, by donors and by the independent research and development provisions of RAND's contracts for the operation of its U.S. Department of Defense (DoD) federally funded research and development centers.

This paper should be of interest to the national security community in the United States and, though written from a U.S. perspective, in allied capitals. It should also promote and inform broader public debate in Europe and the United States.

RAND Project AIR FORCE

RAND Project AIR FORCE (PAF), a division of the RAND Corporation, is the U.S. Air Force's federally funded research and development center for studies and analyses. PAF provides the Air Force with independent analyses of policy alternatives affecting the development, employment, combat readiness, and support of current and future aerospace forces. Research is conducted in four programs: Force Modernization and Employment; Manpower, Personnel, and Training; Resource Management; and Strategy and Doctrine.

Additional information about PAF is available on our Web site:
http://www.rand.org/paf

Contents

Preface ... iii
Tables ... vii
Summary ... ix
Acknowledgments ... xiii
Abbreviations ... xv

CHAPTER ONE
Introduction ... 1
Why Rewrite the Strategic Concept? ... 1
Balancing Strategic Flexibility and Coherence ... 2
Outline of This Paper ... 2

CHAPTER TWO
Direction 1: Refocus on Europe ... 5
Strategic Rationale ... 5
Basic Military Implications ... 5
Main Challenges ... 6
Assessment ... 6

CHAPTER THREE
Direction 2: A New Focus on the Greater Middle East ... 9
Strategic Rationale ... 9
Basic Military Implications ... 9
Main Challenges ... 10
Assessment ... 11

CHAPTER FOUR
Direction 3: A Focus on Fragile States ... 13
Strategic Rationale ... 13
Basic Military Implications ... 13
Main Challenges ... 14
Assessment ... 15

CHAPTER FIVE
Direction 4: A Focus on Nonstate Threats ... 17
Strategic Rationale ... 17

Basic Military Implications 17
Main Challenges 18
NATO and Cyberwar: Illustrative Requirements 18
Assessment 19

CHAPTER SIX
Direction 5: A Global Alliance of Liberal Democracies 21
Strategic Rationale 21
Basic Military Implications 21
Main Challenges 23
Assessment 23

CHAPTER SEVEN
Conclusions 25
Refocus on Europe, Focus on Nonstate Threats, and Focus on Fragile States 25
Refocus on Europe, Focus on Nonstate Threats, and Focus on the Greater Middle East 26
Refocus on Europe and Focus on Nonstate Threats 26
Refocus on Europe and Focus on the Greater Middle East 26
Refocus on Europe, Focus on the Greater Middle East, Focus on Fragile States, and Focus on Nonstate Threats 26
Moving Forward 27

APPENDIX
Summary Tables 29

Bibliography 33

Tables

A.1. Central Threats and Problems, Compared by Perception 29
A.2. Main Implications of Each Direction 30

Summary

To address the security challenges it faces, the United States will need the active support of its allies. This means, in particular, ensuring that the states joined in NATO remain able and willing to make a contribution to resolving their common security problems wherever possible. The current revision of NATO's strategic concept offers an excellent opportunity to further this aim. It is a chance to build consensus about the future and thereby steer the alliance in a direction that will help keep it relevant.

The alliance has long provided its member states with considerable power and influence in world affairs. It offers the citizens of its member states a level of confidence that they will live their lives in peace and with security. It is a cornerstone of the transatlantic relationship and a repository of members' shared history. For all these reasons, an effort to sustain the alliance is worthwhile. Recent years, however, have seen strategic drift within the alliance and disagreements over its basic purposes. The revision of the strategic concept must, on the most basic level, revitalize the alliance by defining a suitable set of purposes that it will serve in the future.

This paper is a contribution to this effort. It examines five possible directions—refocus on Europe, new focus on the greater Middle East, focus on fragile states, focus on nonstate threats, and a global alliance of liberal democracies—for the alliance in the next ten to 15 years, assessing them against certain key political and military criteria. The purpose is to offer those involved in the rewrite both a range of potential options and a preliminary assessment of the feasibility and potential implications of each. In contrast with the revision process, which will invariably begin with the political and bureaucratic constraints the alliance faces and work within these, we attempt a fresh, bottom-up look at what NATO might do, then examine benefits and drawbacks, including political constraints.

What Are Some of the Key Benefits and Problems of Each of the Five Directions?

Refocus on Europe

There are several reasons the alliance might choose to refocus on Europe. One is uncertainty regarding the future course of Russian foreign and security policy; another is continued instability in the Balkans; and a third is the fact that NATO's ability to serve European security is well proven. A return to Europe might provide relief from Afghanistan and signal a period of regeneration for the alliance. There is no doubt that NATO can be effective in Europe. There is one major problem, however, with this direction: There is little in it for the United States.

Indeed, if NATO were to return to Europe, the United States could gradually lose interest in the alliance, undermining its credibility over time. While the strategic concept will surely want to reflect NATO's continued commitment to European security, it will need to do far more. (See pp. 5–8.)

New Focus on the Greater Middle East

An alternative direction that has been considered in the past, but never fully developed, is a new focus on the greater Middle East, or, as the French have called it, the "zone of crisis" that stretches from the Sahara through Pakistan. Here is the area of the world where the most threats to allied security originate, be they threats to allied nations' energy supplies, threats from terrorist groups, or threats from the proliferation of ballistic missiles and nuclear weapons. From the perspective of classical alliance theory, the Middle East is the obvious place to focus the alliance. Unfortunately, the political difficulties that any such focus would involve are manifold and may be so great as to be prohibitive. A NATO focused on peaceful change in the Middle East may not be a realistic option. This fact, however, points to the inherent challenge of finding a meaningful focus for NATO: If the alliance cannot serve the interests of its members in the Middle East, maintaining the alliance's vitality may prove difficult. (See pp. 9–12.)

Focus on Fragile States

Another direction the alliance might adopt involves fragile and failed states. It is now widely, though not unanimously, agreed that failed states are the wellspring of several of the forces that threaten allied security today. NATO, moreover, is currently involved in an extensive effort to strengthen the fragile Afghanistan state. If the allies fail there, there may be little point in considering other directions, given the impact that failure would have on U.S. attitudes toward the alliance. A strategic concept that focused attention on the problem of failed states would simply be a recognition of a major task that NATO has already undertaken and would be beneficial for this reason alone. The difficulties the alliance has encountered in Afghanistan, however, are precisely those it might encounter in making failed states a major future focus. Nevertheless, not doing so could have serious consequences for allied unity. (See pp. 13–16.)

Focus on Nonstate Threats

A fourth direction includes nonstate threats. Just as most security analysts now recognize the importance of failed states, most also recognize the importance of nonstate threats. NATO could choose to give new emphasis to nonstate and so-called hybrid threats, such as terrorism, cyberthreats, piracy, or even environmental disasters. Doing so would imply a significant shift in the nature of the alliance, which to date has largely prepared itself to counter state-based threats. NATO would take a further step toward becoming a security *organization* rather than a traditional security *alliance*. Although these are not mutually exclusive concepts, they are different in character. The main challenge would be in achieving this transformation and ensuring the cooperation it requires on such issues as law enforcement and intelligence sharing. (See pp. 17–20.)

Global Alliance of Liberal Democracies

Finally, the alliance might choose to go global, affirming its core values rather than its traditional regional identity, and extending offers of membership to liberal democracies around the world. This direction is indeed radical but has been raised in a number of variations in the past decade. It is largely unrealistic, however, given not only the financial costs implied but also the fact that it is unclear who would actually want to join a global NATO in the first place. Hence, while the strategic concept will have to reflect a global vision that recognizes that NATO is part of a global security environment—a fact that entails developing more-effective relations with partners around the world—it should not strive to become a global alliance in the strict sense. (See pp. 21–24.)

What Combination of These Directions Is Best?

Refocus on Europe, Focus on Nonstate Threats, and Focus on Fragile States

One model would be to combine a refocus on Europe with a focus on fragile and failed states. This would respond to the current imperative of success in Afghanistan without neglecting European security. This model might be made more attractive by combining it with the non-state direction. The three together could allow an alliance that is flexible enough to meet future contingencies yet not vague or incoherent. (See p. 25.)

Refocus on Europe and Focus on the Greater Middle East

Alternatively, the alliance might choose to focus on the Middle East and Europe and work to overcome the political obstacles to a new focus on the Middle East. This focus would have the benefit of geographical coherence and would serve the interests of nearly all the members while allowing continued focus on Afghanistan. (See p. 26.)

Moving Forward

Other combinations are also possible and examined in Chapter Seven, but combining all the directions would deprive the strategic concept of coherence and is thus to be avoided. Unfortunately, the strategic concept that emerges may well attempt to do so. If this turns out to be the case, it will be essential to identify clear priorities, leaving some directions for the distant future while establishing others as critical missions for the next decade.

Revising the strategic concept will be a challenging process that will ultimately require a combination of creative, problem-focused leadership and skilled diplomatic deal-brokering among the allies. It is a challenge worth taking up, however, for the member states and for the broader transatlantic relationship.

Acknowledgments

I thank the several RAND researchers who supported and participated in the discussions on which this paper is based. I also thank Joya Laha for her valuable assistance in putting it together.

Abbreviations

C2	command and control
C4ISR	command, control, communications, computers, intelligence, surveillance, and reconnaissance
COIN	counterinsurgency
DoD	U.S. Department of Defense
EU	European Union
GDP	gross domestic product
ISAF	International Security Assistance Force
NAC	North Atlantic Council
NATO	North Atlantic Treaty Organization
NTM-A	North Atlantic Treaty Organization Training Mission–Afghanistan
NTM-I	North Atlantic Treaty Organization Training Mission–Iraq
OMLT	operational mentor and liaison team
PAF	RAND Project AIR FORCE
PRT	provincial reconstruction team
SSR	security-sector reform
UN	United Nations
WMD	weapons of mass destruction

CHAPTER ONE

Introduction

Why Rewrite the Strategic Concept?

Two decades after the end of the Cold War, the North Atlantic Treaty Organization faces a security environment that, while radically changed in nature, remains daunting and complex. To make matters worse, economic forces could aggravate many challenges while simultaneously constraining allies' means of addressing them. In these circumstances, the importance of working with allies to manage and mitigate their common security problems is paramount. Absent the overweening threat of the Soviet Union, however, allied cooperation has grown less certain. NATO must thus strive persistently to ensure that it remains useful and relevant and that member states share a broadly common vision of their major security challenges. Building strategic consensus and thereby ensuring that NATO remains relevant should be the basic aim in rewriting the NATO strategic concept.

The strategic concept is NATO's core strategy document. The last formal revision took place in 1999 (see NATO, 1999). Since then, the international security environment has changed a great deal. The allies face several new threats—notably, though not solely, al Qaeda. At the same time, a number of older security problems persist. Meanwhile, and in consequence, the dimensions of warfare have expanded to include, for example, irregular warfare. Although periodic NATO summits have produced communiqués that partially account for these changes—most recently the Declaration on Alliance Security produced at the Strasbourg-Kehl summit in April 2009 (NATO, 2009)—the need for a thorough revision of the strategic concept is widely recognized.

Secretary General Anders Fogh Rasmussen has outlined an inclusive process that the strategic-concept revision will follow. A group of experts has been named that will meet periodically to prepare a report on the strategic concept, to be delivered in the spring of 2010. That report should then serve as a draft and basis for negotiations, to be led by Rasmussen in the second half of 2010. A parallel process of public consultation through a series of seminars began in July 2009 and will also inform the debate. There are already several expert reports available on the subject, many of which figure in the bibliography of this paper.

The strategic concept is not binding and thus cannot prescribe NATO's future, but the revision offers an excellent opportunity to stimulate productive debate and thereby reenergize and refocus the alliance on members' common problems and their possible solutions. The model for the expert group is the Cold War Harmel report (NATO, 1967 [2000]), although its transformative results may prove difficult to replicate for several reasons. Building consensus among 28 member states will not be easy, and there are limitations to what the revision can achieve. But the effort is worthwhile and overdue. A vital NATO can offer its members enhanced peace, security, and influence in the world. It also serves as a cornerstone of the transatlantic relationship. These are worth working to sustain.

Balancing Strategic Flexibility and Coherence

Ideally, the strategic concept would outline a single coherent vision of NATO's purposes and the basic strategies by which it intends to pursue those purposes. To be meaningful, this vision would be more specific than simply stating that the alliance will defend the interests of its members. While this is an accurate statement of the alliance's fundamental aims, it has limited value when it comes to generating the will to act. To the extent possible, therefore, the strategic concept should be truly conceptual and not just a laundry list of particular desires and individual intentions of NATO member states.

Achieving this, however, will not be easy, and there are downsides to conceptual economy and elegance. Given uncertainty about the future, the strategic concept should aim to be relevant for the next decade. Even with this time horizon, however, some degree of flexibility will help to ensure a longer shelf life and leave room for ad hoc adaptation. Similarly, to satisfy a sufficient number of divergent member concerns, a multiplicity of stated aims may be necessary.

Nevertheless, the alliance cannot be all things to all members. Too much flexibility or too far-reaching a set of tasks will deprive the strategic concept of coherence and thus its usefulness as a means of building momentum for concrete action. Achieving a suitable balance between strategic ambiguity and coherence will thus be key. Insofar as the alliance can define meaningful common problems, it should seek to do so. This is, after all, what makes the strategic concept a "concept" and not simply a list of threats or aspirations.

It is also important to note that the process of the rewrite may matter more than the final document itself, given that it is uncertain how much the strategic concept actually influences NATO policy, especially in a crisis. The strategic concept is not a binding document but rather a philosophical statement of intent, designed as much for consumption outside the alliance as for internal guidance. It does affect allied defense planning and is significant for the NATO bureaucracy and hence day-to-day operations, but, because many future security threats are unknown today, even if the strategic concept were a binding document, it could be overtaken by events. A case in point is the fact that the 1999 document made only passing reference to terrorism.

Outline of This Paper

To help stimulate debate during the revision process, this paper examines five possible directions for the alliance. The directions represent the author's understanding of the major options on the table. Although they reflect different strategic priorities and entail different military requirements, they are not distinct, and some will need to be combined in the final document. The author also does not endorse them all equally. Each raises a different set of problems. The possible directions are

- refocus on Europe
- a new focus on the greater Middle East

- a focus on fragile states
- a focus on nonstate threats
- a global alliance of liberal democracies.

The paper examines each possible direction in turn. The method is dialectical, first laying out the positive case for it and then offering critical analysis. In each case, the discussion

- describes the basic strategic rationale for the direction
- outlines illustrative military requirements
- examines the main political and military challenges
- offers a brief overall assessment.

It is important to note that the order in which these directions are presented is not intended to indicate preference.

A concluding section briefly outlines the implications of the analysis and explores some possible models for combining the directions in the strategic concept. An appendix of summary tables and a bibliography may be found at the end of the paper.

CHAPTER TWO

Direction 1: Refocus on Europe

Strategic Rationale

In several European capitals, there is a growing—though by no means dominant—chorus of voices who would like to see NATO refocus on Europe.

Although NATO has gone out of area repeatedly since the end of the Cold War, these missions have proven more and more challenging for the alliance as their distance from Brussels increases. Meanwhile, the Balkans—especially Kosovo, but also Bosnia and Herzegovina and even Macedonia—continue to evince often troubling levels of instability.

Moreover, Russia's future appears increasingly uncertain. Although Russia is not a major security threat, its recent invasion of Georgia creates obvious problems for the alliance. On the one hand, there are good reasons for NATO to seek closer cooperation with Russia on security and other issues. Russia is an important player in the politics and diplomacy of security in the Balkans, South Asia, and Middle East—regions of central concern to NATO member states. Russian cooperation is needed on many nontraditional threats, such as the proliferation of weapons of mass destruction (WMD) and terrorism. Better relations with Russia could also help allay the concerns of NATO members once under the Soviet yoke.

On the other hand, the current trajectory of Russian policy does not tend to facilitate a relaunch of Russia-NATO relations. Russia has admitted no guilt over its recent invasion of Georgia, is making plans for a long-term military presence in Abkhazia, and claims a right to a sphere of influence around its borders. That Russia should have some influence with its neighbors is natural, but this does not amount to a prerogative for interfering directly in their domestic politics, let alone invading them. Even if Russia does not intend for this prerogative to extend to central and eastern Europe, the possibility that it might do so is clearly cause for great concern in several of NATO's new member states: A Russian military incursion into eastern Europe, even if small in scale and ultimately a military failure, could create enormous problems for the alliance.

Given these problems, a return to Europe is worth serious consideration.

Basic Military Implications

A refocus on European security would include hard and soft dimensions. On the soft side, the alliance would deepen ties with Russia in an effort to ease tensions and increase mutual security. This would be a primarily political and diplomatic initiative, including reinvigorating and possibly upgrading the NATO-Russia Council while encouraging President Dmitriy

Anatolyevich Medvedev's views on European security to be voiced in an appropriate, constructive venue. A soft strategy might also involve joint military exercises and extending existing military-to-military exchanges and liaisons. NATO could meanwhile become a forum for the negotiation of joint reductions in member-state nuclear arsenals, in the context of a broader East-West disarmament agreement.

It should be noted that this vision might, in the near term at least, imply a temporary freeze on further enlargement. Although enlargement does not, in fact, threaten Russia, it has become an impediment to improvements in NATO-Russia relations and thus would work directly against a relaunch of Russia-NATO ties.

On the hard side, the alliance would preserve a capability for conventional and nuclear deterrence, both as a safeguard against a deterioration in NATO-Russia relations and as a means of responding to the threat posed by nuclear-armed regional powers, such as Iran. The latter might entail a review of NATO's nuclear posture. NATO would also maintain its ability to conduct stabilization operations in the event of a relapse in the Balkans, although this possibility is now increasingly remote.

NATO would also undertake new defense initiatives in some eastern European member states to increase the credibility of Article V of the North Atlantic Treaty (NATO, 1949) and ensure that any Russian provocations in eastern Europe—however unlikely—are effectively deterred. Such initiatives, however, would have to be undertaken with full respect for the Russia-NATO Founding Act (NATO, 1997 [2002]) if they are not to undermine Russia-NATO relations.

Main Challenges

NATO is very well suited to conduct the missions that a strategic concept focused on territorial threats to Europe would involve and is already prepared for or conducting most of them. The only area in which NATO might encounter difficulty is in increasing the credibility of its deterrent for certain new member states. At present, of course, NATO does not deploy forces against any country, including Russia, and has no operational planning for military conflict with Russia in the Baltic states or anywhere else. If it desired to increase the credibility of its conventional deterrent in the Baltics, for example, this would be possible but would require significant military investments, and these could meet political objections and possibly further exacerbate relations with Russia.

Assessment

In political terms, refocusing NATO on Europe would no doubt be the lowest cost of the options examined herein. The problem is that it does little to encourage NATO allies to work with the United States to resolve its most pressing common security problems. Russia's future is uncertain, and Russia is a major foreign-policy challenge for NATO members, but this fact must not be confused with the security threat that Russia poses to the alliance, which is at present comparatively small for member states. Despite its possession of a nuclear arsenal and increases in defense spending, Russia's conventional forces remain subpar, especially by Western standards. Russia can threaten Europe's energy supplies, sow political discord within the alliance, and undertake a range of other nonmilitary activities that create problems for the United States and Europe. The majority of these problems, however, are not problems that NATO, as a military alliance, is well suited to counter. If NATO were to make countering Russia's manipulation of energy supplies a mission, for example, what countermeasures would it propose to employ? The most obvious would be economic sanctions, but such measures are far better suited to the European Union (EU).

Moreover, a refocus on Europe would, in certain respects, be an admission of defeat for NATO in Afghanistan and would raise serious questions about NATO's ability to serve major U.S. needs. NATO obviously would still continue as an institution that added value to security in Europe, but its value to the United States would be diminished, even from its already reduced status in post–Cold War U.S. strategy. Over time, the recognition of waning U.S. interest in the alliance could discredit the U.S. security guarantee to Europe, undermining the fundamental justification for starting down this path in the first place.

To be sure, NATO continues to play a useful role stabilizing Europe—in the Balkans in particular. It is, of course, difficult to identify exactly the degree to which NATO's contributes to European security, given that its contribution is closely linked—indeed, in many ways, inextricably so—to the stability provided by the EU. Nevertheless, it is likely that, if NATO were absent from Europe, instability would increase, especially around the alliance's borders and in some new member states.

To point out that a refocus on Europe is a nonstarter is in no way meant to argue that NATO should withdraw from Europe. To the contrary, if NATO is not strong in Europe, it will not be strong elsewhere. However, an alliance focused narrowly on Europe could give rise to a gradual U.S. disengagement from NATO over time and, ultimately, undermine the credibility of alliance itself. This would serve no one, including those members that might, in principle, be most interested in returning NATO to its European roots.

CHAPTER THREE

Direction 2: A New Focus on the Greater Middle East

Strategic Rationale

NATO allies share major interests in the greater Middle East, the region that stretches from the Sahara to Pakistan. A new focus on the greater Middle East would develop NATO resources in support of the shared goals of defeating al Qaeda, managing the Iranian nuclear threat, and ensuring the flow of energy from the Persian Gulf. It would also permit continued focus on Afghanistan.

If alliances are based on interests, the greater Middle East is where the most common interests of NATO's members are threatened, and it thus makes sense that NATO should focus on it. Member states' interests in the region are obviously not identical, and preferred strategies differ, sometimes greatly. Whereas concern about al Qaeda is somewhat less in European countries than in the United States, European interest in securing the region's energy reserves and defusing the threat of a nuclear Iran is at least as great as that of the United States. The broad, shared imperative of thwarting threats from the region is clear.

Given NATO's image in the region and the likely objections of some member states to involving NATO more deeply there, NATO would have to pursue a dual, long-term strategy for helping foster peaceful change with stability. NATO would not seek to become the only or even the primary international organization active in the region. Instead, it would seek to gradually become the lead institution for the security and defense aspects of a broader regional transformation in which other actors, especially the EU, are also engaged.

Drawing, for example, on the success of the Partnership for Peace program, NATO could significantly deepen its relationship with the Middle East. There would be resistance at first, but, over time, the benefits of working with NATO would grow clearer. NATO could expand, deepen, and reenergize its existing regional partnerships, bringing more financial means and security expertise to bear on the problems these states face while promoting a regional system of collective security. It would work closely with other actors, especially the EU.

At the same time, in the tradition of defense and détente, NATO would retain its capacity for military intervention. NATO would also reassess its nuclear posture and would develop contingency plans for a deterrent against ballistic-missile threats from the region.

Basic Military Implications

To be most effective, this focus would require hard and soft security dimensions. The soft security dimension, which could take center stage, would involve

- an in-depth assessment of the Partnership for Peace process and an effort to combine the lessons learned with an assessment of the needs of major Middle Eastern states and development of effective partnership models on this basis
- training and equipping regional states for peacekeeping and peace-support operations and to facilitate interoperability to a NATO standard for joint operations
- using the partnerships to deepen cultural exchanges and develop cross-cultural awareness within military officer corps
- regional discussions of security issues to build collective security in the region
- working closely with other regional actors, especially the EU, to coordinate NATO's security activities with a broader political strategy for regional change.

A new focus on the Middle East would also imply maintaining a continually evolving hard security capability for the region, specifically

- the ability to project power to conduct major combat operations in the region
- continued efforts to improve allied interoperability to ensure this capability and corresponding investments in allied command, control, communications, computers, intelligence, surveillance, and reconnaissance (C4ISR)
- continued modernization of European militaries and further allied efforts to this end, especially through Allied Command Transformation and the NATO Response Force
- the ability to project power for smaller-scale, special operations, and appropriate NATO command capabilities
- reinforcement of extended deterrence to counter moves toward nuclearization by existing NATO members (e.g., Turkey)
- efforts to ensure that NATO decisionmakers have a range of response options available to increase the credibility of NATO's deterrent
- continued development of missile-defense capabilities, both at the theater and strategic levels—although it should be noted that there is continued disagreement over the potential effectiveness of missile defenses against an enemy armed with more than a very small number of ballistic missiles
- use of the new partnerships to improve access to regional assets for logistics and supply.

Main Challenges

Increasing NATO's focus on the Middle East does not involve any major new military challenges. It implies the development of some new capabilities within NATO—for example, enhanced institutional capabilities for managing allied security-sector reform (SSR) initiatives. Developing such capabilities, however, is probably a good idea anyway, given that NATO can maintain a continuity in SSR that the lead-nation or bilateral approach often lacks. It can also draw on a broader array of national expertise than any individual nation. Eastern European states, which have recently undergone their own reforms, could prove a valuable resource for a Partnership for Peace–like initiative in the region, even in states with cultures that differ from their own, provided that the initiative is not applied in a cookie-cutter fashion but with a recognition of the fact that the states themselves are different and that NATO's objectives in eastern Europe and the Middle East differ.

Assuming that an adoption of this direction implies the political will to ensure that European militaries continue to transform for deployability (and implies corresponding levels of European defense spending), NATO would be well prepared to meet the requirements of the hard, defense side of the military strategy. Provided that the current operational tempo declines and the economic crisis does not worsen significantly, NATO should still be able to project formidable military forces to the region as a credible foundation for this initiative.

Without political will, of course, NATO could well fall short on military needs, and, politically, the obstacles to any new NATO initiative in the region are considerable. Despite the fact that most European states face greater threats from the Middle East than from within Europe itself, this focus would invariably raise issues.

First, objections both within the alliance and in the region could arise if the new focus is seen as a U.S. attempt to transform NATO into a tool of U.S. policy against Iran. It is important, however, to note that the depth of these objections could depend a great deal on context. In the event of a significant improvement in U.S.-Iran relations, objections might be less strident, and a NATO focus on the Middle East could become a natural complement to improving U.S.-Iran relations if it served to reassure other regional powers. European objections might be alleviated by an explicit rejection of preemptive war and corresponding language in the strategic concept.

Second, and of no less importance, NATO could discover that few Middle Eastern states are interested in becoming NATO partners. NATO's prestige in the region, which was low to begin with, has declined further due to negative perceptions of the International Security Assistance Force (ISAF), and this might further discourage regional enthusiasm for the new initiatives. Designing the right partner packages—with adequate financial and other incentives—would therefore be crucial.

Third, it would be very important to ensure equality among partners and avoid any signs of favoritism that might undermine the basic peace-building purpose of the initiative.

Assessment

Encouraging a new allied focus on the Middle East would directly benefit a wide range of major U.S. and European security problems. NATO is also militarily capable of realizing it, provided political will. Unfortunately, the political issues it raises are very real. The faltering of NATO's existing initiatives in the region is testimony to this fact.

In other words, NATO is unlikely to be able to agree to the very direction that seems most logical objectively. This is in itself problematic for the alliance: If NATO is unable to develop its strategic relationship with the one region where there is the greatest consonance of interests among NATO member states, the vitality of the alliance can only suffer.

CHAPTER FOUR

Direction 3: A Focus on Fragile States

Strategic Rationale

Since the end of the Cold War, the problems created by failed and fragile states have repeatedly led to military interventions. They are likely to do so again, whether for humanitarian reasons, as in Darfur, or for narrower security reasons, as in Somalia. The burdens of these interventions will obviously be more evenly shared if they are undertaken under a NATO rather than U.S. or coalition-of-the-willing format. With NATO, such interventions may also be more effective for political reasons.

By focusing on state fragility, the alliance would work to develop robust capabilities for effective intervention in failed states whenever NATO leaders deem it necessary. A NATO focus on fragile states would not mean that NATO would be the only international organization with capabilities in this area, nor that NATO would undertake to intervene in all fragile states, nor that NATO would undertake the diplomatic, economic, or political tasks now recognized as crucial for successful nation-building. An expansion of efforts on these nonmilitary aspects of the problem would be a logical complement to this change in NATO's focus, but, to avoid the appearance of competition with the EU, NATO might limit itself to security tasks, coordinating its work with the EU and other actors.

Focusing NATO explicitly on fragile states would have the major benefit of being directly relevant to stabilizing Afghanistan and ensuring against a reemergence of a regime sympathetic to al Qaeda. Developing these capabilities could also better prepare the alliance to respond in the face of a deterioration of Pakistan. This focus would put pressure on allies to develop the capabilities for complex stabilization operations while encouraging the alliance to develop a consensus on crucial strategic questions and the resource commitments they require.

Basic Military Implications

This focus also implies hard and soft security dimensions. On the soft side, it must be noted, many of these steps could be taken in close coordination with the EU. Specifically, NATO would do the following:

- Take proactive steps to bolster stability in states at risk of collapse, particularly through SSR and security-force assistance and training, as it is currently doing in Afghanistan (NATO Training Mission–Afghanistan, or NTM-A) and Iraq (NTM-I).
- Establish mechanisms for integrating non-NATO partner countries into NATO missions in failed states. These partnerships could be permanent or bounded by the terms of

specific missions. In either case, it will be necessary not only to ensure smooth operating arrangements with partners making military contributions to NATO efforts but also to negotiate agreements to provide partners with appropriate political representation at the North Atlantic Council (NAC).

- Fix the broken EU-NATO working relationship and ensure that NATO and the EU remain complementary institutions.
- Continue to develop the comprehensive approach, including through a concerted effort to improve operational mentor and liaison teams (OMLTs) and provincial reconstruction teams (PRTs).
- Formally integrate civilian-military capabilities into allied defense planning.

The hard side of this focus would involve the following:

- Agree to a comprehensive counterinsurgency (COIN) strategy and commit the resources needed to make it effective.
- Maintain the ability to sustain a corps-size peacekeeping force for one to two years at significant distances from the North Atlantic region.
- Continue to rely on special forces for many kinetic operations, with adequate NATO special operations command structures.
- Possibly reduce the size of NATO nuclear forces, as well as forces designed for traditional state-state major combat, such as heavy armor.

Main Challenges

Stabilizing and rebuilding war-torn states has historically proven extremely difficult. Provided adequate political will, however, the military challenges involved in operationalizing a focus on failed and fragile states are at least no greater for NATO than for any other organization. Indeed, NATO has already begun to develop many of the capabilities required as a result of operations in the Balkans and Afghanistan. While there have been challenges in all of these cases, the challenges are not of a kind that NATO is militarily unable to overcome. NATO's difficulties in Afghanistan are largely the result of political constraints, strategic missteps, and the inherent difficulty of the mission. They should not be seen as evidence of any inherent allied incapacity.

One exception might be COIN, in which NATO's own lack of know-how has been an obstacle in the past. NATO is far from the only modern military organization that has had difficulty with COIN, however, and, to the extent that COIN operations can be effective, there is no obvious reason that NATO cannot conduct them at least as well as, if not better than, any individual nation. When it comes to other international organizations, NATO is the only institution that will have any capabilities in this area for the foreseeable future.

However, the military costs of nation-building operations alone are very substantial. This is largely due to the fact that these operations are measured in years or even decades and impose a continued operational toll on participating forces. At present, because many of the most important European militaries have been worn down by the current operational tempo, resource shortfalls are apt to continue. Of course, the hope of reducing these shortfalls is the very motive for making fragile states a focus in the first place. Provided such a focus and corresponding defense programming, these shortfalls could be expected to decline over time.

The military challenges of this focus are thus, in principle, no greater than for any other organization and may, in some respects, be less.

The primary challenges would be political. First, the EU considers coping with state fragility a task for which it has a special calling, and some view the United Nations (UN) as the most suitable institution for this task. If NATO develops capabilities for coping with state failure, there will be some overlap with both organizations.

Objectively, this is not problematic. Indeed, the United States often prefers to leave these missions to others or participate in them under a UN or even EU umbrella. The EU and UN, however, will not always be up to the task, and NATO has obvious comparative advantages when it comes to more-challenging missions or more-challenging aspects of stabilization operations, especially COIN. Developing the full gamut of options for policymakers thus implies ensuring that NATO can respond to state fragility when it is called on to do so. The reentrance of France into the NATO military command may make it easier to ensure that politics does not get in the way of developing NATO capabilities for stabilization missions, even in Africa, the region on which the UN and EU have focused historically.

Second, it may be difficult to gain allied agreement to a mission that is geographically open-ended. Constraining the mission to areas in which NATO members share interests might help overcome objections, without imposing explicit limitations. Still, if NATO were excluded from, for example, interventions in Africa, this direction might have relatively little future value in the post-Afghanistan era.

Third, allied experience in Afghanistan could easily end up being the main blockage to developing in this direction. If the experience in Afghanistan is widely viewed as a failure, there is little chance that the allies will agree to undertake another similar mission elsewhere, even if they agreed to the direction in principle.

Assessment

These drawbacks notwithstanding, moving in this direction would have the significant, immediate benefit of focusing allied attention and resources on the war NATO is fighting now. This is a strong argument in itself, given that success in Afghanistan may be necessary to ensure the durability of the alliance as its members know it: While the alliance would probably survive failure in Afghanistan, failure would inevitably reduce U.S. interest in NATO, potentially hollowing it out over time. NATO has been developing its capabilities for dealing with failed states via operational imperative of Afghanistan, and a strategic concept that recognizes this fact is warranted.

CHAPTER FIVE

Direction 4: A Focus on Nonstate Threats

Strategic Rationale

Nonstate threats are growing in importance, and NATO could agree to take major new steps to combat them. Moreover, defense against most nonstate threats requires international cooperation, and NATO, as the world's leading international security organization, is well suited to the task. A NATO focused on nonstate threats could be expected to make a greater contribution to fighting terrorist groups, combating WMD proliferation, defending member states against cyberattacks, and fighting a range of problems stemming from global organized crime. A NATO role in homeland security and disaster management might even be included under this general rubric.

As long as strategies are left relatively open, one of the benefits of this focus is that it should not raise major intra-alliance or geopolitical issues. All members should be able to agree that these threats are serious and recognize that there are benefits to addressing them jointly. At the same time, developing NATO capabilities against nonstate and hybrid threats should not threaten any major state and hence would not raise any geopolitical issues.

Basic Military Implications

Operationalizing a NATO focus on nonstate threats is challenging in at least three ways. First, these threats are evolving, and members are thus continually learning how to combat them effectively. Second, in general, they require substantial coordination both within states and among states. Third, the category is somewhat open-ended, and the appropriate military strategy and requirements are correspondingly broad.

These caveats notwithstanding, this direction would have the following general implications for NATO strategy and military planning:

- NATO would maintain and, to the extent possible, upgrade its capabilities for projecting power on a small scale, especially for special operations.
- NATO would establish mechanisms for closer cooperation with the law-enforcement agencies of member states.
- NATO would enhance efforts at intra-alliance intelligence cooperation against these threats.
- NATO would enhance information exchange within the alliance, especially on border monitoring, tracking, and pursuit activities of allied law-enforcement agencies.

- NATO would develop global partnerships aimed at combating these threats. These global partnerships would differ significantly from previous NATO partnership programs, since their purpose would expressly not be to prepare countries for full membership with an Article V commitment but instead to facilitate information exchange, improve partner border security and the security of WMD materials, and enhance cooperation for monitoring, tracking, and combating nonstate threats.
- NATO would establish standing working groups to develop joint strategies and doctrine for combating these threats.
- NATO would take specific actions to defend its members from nonstate threats—for example, helping member states improve port security and developing other systems to help member states prevent nuclear weapons from entering allied territory through covert means.

Main Challenges

Transforming NATO along these lines would involve a significant shift away from NATO's traditional role as an alliance designed to defeat conventional threats. Accordingly, it might require extensive military reforms. The costs of such reforms, although variable depending on the scope of the strategy adopted, would probably be relatively low, however, since a focus on nonstate and hybrid threats would not involve a major investment in new military hardware. In general, further investment in technology would be expected, and operational costs would be moderate. The emphasis would be on lower levels of highly skilled manpower. Provided that partnership initiatives maintained a focus on nonstate and hybrid threats and did not mutate into partnerships geared to prepare states for full membership, the costs of these partnerships could also be expected to be relatively low. Given declining European defense spending in terms of gross domestic product (GDP), this direction's likely lower costs might also permit each European state to contribute to NATO on a basis commensurate with the size of its economy.

The main military challenge would probably arise from the need to build effective links with member-state law-enforcement agencies. The sheer scale of this challenge, especially given the varied nature of each member state's law-enforcement institutions, is considerable. It is not insurmountable, though, provided that sufficient political will is mobilized and buy-in from law-enforcement agencies is secured.

The investment this direction requires would vary depending on the particular nonstate threats on which NATO decided to focus. One illustrative example is cyberwar.

NATO and Cyberwar: Illustrative Requirements

The threat of damaging cyberattacks is a current concern for all members of the alliance, though to differing degrees. Given the level at which allied communications and economic networks are now interdependent, there is a strong argument to be made for allied unity in defending vulnerable members against cyberattacks. That said, little is known about the extent and nature of the damage that cyberattacks can actually inflict. If NATO chose to become more involved in defending against attacks in cyberspace, a number of options would be available. It could, in particular,

- develop mechanisms to share cyberthreat assessments and tactical warnings within the alliance
- provide technical assistance for members and exchange capabilities
- develop integrated cyberdefense for key allied infrastructures
- develop deterrent or offensive cybercounterstrike capability
- offer extended cyberdeterrence to members and NATO partners.

Taking any of these steps, however, would raise a number of issues, including the following:

- the level of certainty required in attributing an attack to an aggressor. Cyberattacks, like certain types of terrorist attacks, can leave doubt as to their perpetrator, rendering effective response politically difficult.
- how much intelligence and technical expertise the allies would be expected to share
- whether to adopt defense or deterrence as a strategy. Deterrence would imply the development of counterstrike capabilities but could result in a cyber–arms race with unknown consequences.
- for a deterrent strategy, whether it would be explicit or implicit
- the extent to which the alliance would compartmentalize cyberspace. In other words, would a cyberattack ever be grounds for a physical counterstrike? If so, what would the threshold be?

Assessment

In general, the nonstate direction has the benefit of responding to security problems that all members of the alliance face—especially, though not exclusively, the threat posed by al Qaeda and its surrogates. It could be difficult to operationalize, though by no means impossible. It would be more challenging militarily than politically.

The main political objections that would arise would stem from the fact that a focus on nonstate threats diverts NATO from its traditional mission of countering state threats. The reality, however, may well be that the main threats the members of the alliance share are no longer state based and that the transformation of the alliance, even if it implies some diminution of NATO's role, is warranted on these grounds.

It has the drawback of being broad and therefore open to broad interpretation, especially when it comes to whether a defensive or proactive strategy is appropriate. This drawback could also be viewed as a benefit, however, because it leaves open the question of where the alliance will fight these threats and hence may be easier to adopt politically. The openness of the option is also attractive because it maximizes flexibility—a benefit, given that uncertainty and complexity will continue to be features of the security environment.

This direction would, in some respects, involve a more limited mission for NATO and, in other respects, a more extensive one. Needless to say, it would be one of value to the vast majority of NATO members, and for which NATO as the world's leading security organization, is well placed to fulfill. Provided that NATO allies can agree to discuss openly the related strategy issues within NATO, finance NATO's development of NATO's own capabilities, and coordinate domestic law-enforcement agencies and counterterrorism efforts, this direction could prove promising.

CHAPTER SIX

Direction 5: A Global Alliance of Liberal Democracies

Strategic Rationale

By any measure, NATO is modern history's longest-standing military alliance. Arguably, its durability springs from the fact that it is not only a classical alliance of interests but also an alliance rooted in common values. That the alliance endures two decades after the end of the Cold War supports this view. To be effective in the future, the alliance might therefore choose to focus on defending its common values. Doing so in today's context would require putting geography aside and enlarging the alliance to include liberal democratic countries around the globe.

A gradual enlargement of NATO to include Australia, New Zealand, Japan, South Africa, Brazil, India, and other states might also provide a reservoir of legitimacy for interventions that is currently only available through the UN. If NATO defines itself in terms of core values and enlarges to include a membership that is geographically much broader and thereby truly representative of those values, it could also serve to legitimize interventions by its member states. Moreover, taking NATO in this direction would enlarge the military resources on which the alliance can draw and improve the geographical reach of such interventions. In the long term, a global NATO might even serve as a foundation from which to build deterrence against a neo-authoritarian axis or other force that competes with or directly challenges liberal democracy. However unlikely such an axis may be today, its emergence cannot be ruled out in the medium to long term.

If NATO were to adopt this vision for its strategic concept, it would have to make a fundamental choice. It could either remain a primarily military alliance or transform itself into an alliance that is mainly political in nature, with military capabilities provided by intra-alliance coalitions of the willing. An in-between option is also conceivable.

Basic Military Implications

To gauge basic military requirements, it is necessary to define three alternatives. First, NATO enlarges to include several new members with full Article V commitments. Second, it extends partnerships that do not involve Article V commitments but do aim to bring the military capabilities of partner states into the alliance for certain types of operations. Third, NATO enlarges either through partnerships or through full membership but deemphasizes its military function and thereby begins a transformation into a largely political alliance, with some rump military capabilities. Of these three cases, the first would clearly require the most resources, followed by the second and the third.

It goes without saying that the first case implies a truly stupendous resource commitment. Some, but by no means all, of the main requirements would include the following:

- major initiatives to equip new and prospective members and bring them up to NATO standards. The investment required would vary enormously, depending on the size, geographical location, and level of development of the prospective member. For example, Australia would be far less costly than India. Brazil might be somewhere in between.
- extended nuclear deterrence for all members, with a corresponding posture and stockpiles of strategic nuclear weapons
- major investment in strategic transport and power projection to ensure global mobility of NATO forces for conventional deterrence and to provide flexible response, augment the nuclear deterrent, and thereby ensure the credibility of Article V
- long-term programs to train and equip new members and ensure interoperability. These will also vary according to a country's level of development and military traditions.
- a major revision of the NATO command structure that allows the full participation of new members
- new NATO political decisionmaking structures that allow for the full participation of several new members without blocking up the system. This might involve, for example, the establishment of a weighted voting scheme or a directorate with permanent and rotating members.

To avoid some, but not all, of these costs, NATO might decide to extend offers of membership only to countries that are already at or close to NATO military standards (e.g., Australia). In this case, however, NATO could not argue that it represents global democratic values, jeopardizing the basic justification for moving in this direction in the first place, especially when it comes to building a reservoir of legitimacy.

An alternative way of reducing the costs would be to eschew Article V enlargement and significantly develop NATO's global partnerships. This is the second suboption. Some of the main military requirements might be

- the development of new modes of partnership that explicitly do not lead to eventual membership in NATO
- investments in partner capacity
- improvements to interoperability with new partners
- new decisionmaking structures to give partners a political and military voice in those NATO operations in which they chose to participate.

In a third suboption, the military requirements are minimal, since, here, the alliance becomes a largely political institution. The main focus would be on NATO political structures to make much broader membership effective.

Main Challenges

Based on the foregoing discussion, the military challenges that these cases would pose are clear. In the first case, the challenge of providing credible, extended deterrence around the world, the financial cost of equipping several new members to NATO standards, and the implications for NATO command and control (C2) would alone be so great as to be difficult to imagine in any but the longest-term time frame. In the second case, the requirements do not differ in general terms from the partnership requirements outlined in some of the other options and, hence, are somewhat easier to conceive, although, depending on specific modalities, they could still be challenging. In the third case, there are no military challenges, since NATO would no longer really be a military alliance.

The political challenges involved in adopting this direction are also very substantial. First, any of the suboptions are very likely to elicit resistance from other members of the alliance, not only among new members but among Europe's major continental powers and possibly Canada.

Second, and of no less importance, it is very uncertain whether other democratic states desire to join NATO in the first place. Some states, such as Australia, seem open to the idea of membership, but only along the lines of the first suboption, in which they share the same rights and military commitments as existing NATO members. In other words, those states that are most likely to bring added value to the alliance are likely to consider joining it only in the most demanding case. On the other end of the scale, countries like India may not be interested in joining NATO under any circumstances whatsoever.

Third, while the financial costs of the first suboption cannot be determined in any rigorous way, they would obviously be extremely high, unless only rich countries that can pay their own way are allowed to join.

Fourth, opening NATO's door globally to democratic states could create a rush for membership among states whose democratic credentials are uncertain, since NATO membership would burnish the democratic credentials of those states that were invited to join. This would pose a difficult challenge to NATO and could easily become a distraction from more-pressing, current NATO missions.

Fifth, the option raises geopolitical issues. The question that would, and has, been raised regarding a NATO that is explicitly global is this: Who or what is it an alliance against? While NATO members might insist that it is not an alliance against any state, there is no way to guarantee that those states that are left out will not see it as an alliance directed against them and take steps to defend themselves or stop NATO from successfully globalizing.

Sixth, although the general nature of this option makes it moderately beneficial to many security challenges, in the near and medium term, a global NATO would be of limited value in meeting pressing, concrete challenges, such as combating al Qaeda and succeeding in Afghanistan.

Assessment

In short, while there is a plausible philosophical rationale for this direction, it would involve serious political and geopolitical challenges and would not do much to address pressing current problems that NATO faces. Moreover, for the version that would be most beneficial, the costs would also be prohibitively high. It is thus unrealistic, whatever its theoretical appeal.

It should be emphasized, however, that most of the other directions examined in this paper imply some extension of NATO's reach through partnerships. These partnerships will differ in substance from the partnerships that a global NATO implies, since they will be focused on specific concrete problems rather than objectives of a more universal nature and would not imply Article V commitments. It may be helpful to maintain this clear distinction during negotiations.

CHAPTER SEVEN

Conclusions

The difficulties raised in the foregoing analysis should serve as a healthy reminder of the challenges NATO faces in revising its strategic concept. The differences in strategic vision, not only between the United States and Europe but also within Europe itself, make the task of identifying an intellectually coherent vision for the alliance extremely challenging. Clearly, no one of the directions outlined here will alone suffice. Some combination will be necessary. Yet, each direction poses problems, and, while more directions means more opportunities for bargains within the alliance, going in several directions at once also means a greater overall number of challenges as well as a risk of incoherence and strategic drift.

Given this, the greatest overarching challenge could in fact become sustaining U.S. commitment to NATO in the long term. Since the 1990s, the implicit bargain at the heart of the strategic concept has been continued U.S. military engagement in Europe in exchange for allied support out of area. After nearly five years of faltering NATO engagement in Afghanistan, this bargain looks increasingly one sided from a U.S. perspective. The problem is all the more acute given the fact that many NATO allies fighting in Afghanistan are doing so at significant domestic political cost and, in contrast with observers in the United States, view their contributions as not only significant but near-maximal. (Here, Germany is a case in point.) While there is little chance that the United States will disengage from European security in the foreseeable future, especially given continued uncertainty about Russia, benign neglect is possible. NATO will never serve all U.S. interests that remain global, but it must serve at least a few important ones to remain viable.

The optimal strategic concept will therefore combine a few of the directions examined here in a way that leaves sufficient flexibility for the unknown while garnering concrete commitments that will diminish the chances of further strategic drift. Which combinations are worth considering?

Refocus on Europe, Focus on Nonstate Threats, and Focus on Fragile States

A first model would combine a refocus on Europe, a new attention to nonstate threats, and a focus on state fragility. This would respond to the current imperative of success in Afghanistan without neglecting European security. Given that the alliance is likely to remain engaged in Afghanistan for the foreseeable future, it seems the most promising bargain. It would require, at a minimum, a renewed commitment to ISAF—so far, a hard sell. However, it would be flexible enough to meet future contingencies yet not so vague as to be incoherent.

Refocus on Europe, Focus on Nonstate Threats, and Focus on the Greater Middle East

A second model would involve interpreting a refocus on European security broadly, to incorporate not only nonstate threats but also threats to Europe emanating from regions nearby—in other words, some combination of the Europe, nonstate, and Middle East options. Such a combination would have the benefit of reassuring new member states that NATO's core is still in Europe while encouraging a greater attention to nuclear proliferation in the Middle East, cyberthreats, and terrorism—issues of significant interest to the United States. The Middle East focus could make this model more ambitious, however, than the first model.

Refocus on Europe and Focus on Nonstate Threats

A third, less ambitious model would just combine the Europe direction and the nonstate direction. On the positive side, this model would emphasize the changing nature of the security problems that NATO allies face and assert NATO's determination to adapt to the new security environment. European allies would agree, in principle, to allowing NATO a greater role in fighting terrorism, expanding its links to law enforcement, and agreeing to the possibility of preparing NATO for counterterrorism missions abroad, at least on a small scale. In addition, European states would agree to the development of new, non–Article V partnerships aimed at combating nonstate threats and building a web of cooperation that extends well beyond NATO's traditional remit. The downside, in addition to those noted in the discussion of the nonstate direction in Chapter Five, would be that it leaves the Afghanistan problem unresolved.

Refocus on Europe and Focus on the Greater Middle East

A fourth, somewhat simpler, though no less ambitious, model would forgo the transformations implied in dealing with nonstate threats and focus NATO simply on the Middle East and Europe. This model would offer geographical coherence, although the political difficulties involved with the Middle East direction would require a longer-term effort. The basic bargain would be the following: In exchange for sustained and even increased U.S. attention to Europe's security problems, European states would be expected to continue to invest in both hard and soft military capabilities, give full political support to NATO peace-building in the Middle East, fully support the development of missile defense within NATO, and agree to discuss and develop a NATO strategy for dealing with nuclear threats from the region.

Refocus on Europe, Focus on the Greater Middle East, Focus on Fragile States, and Focus on Nonstate Threats

The fifth, most ambitious alternative is the gourmand model. Here NATO goes in all directions at once—with the exception of global NATO. This may well be the model that emerges, both to maintain flexibility and to accommodate the interests and views of all the members.

Such a model, however, risks continued strategic drift, unless it is the product of a genuine commitment to far-reaching transformation on the part of all allies, a transformation that goes beyond the wording of national security strategies to include increases in defense spending and reallocation of defense resources.

Moving Forward

Whatever the shape of the strategic concept that emerges, it will not be permanent. The process of the rewrite, however, is still a chance to build consensus within the alliance about the main threats its members face. As the global economic crisis increases pressure on allied defense budgets, it may become even more difficult to gain meaningful commitments from allies to sustain their military forces at current levels. But this is all the more reason to seize the rewrite as an opportunity to press the alliance to put the resources it does have to meet the security challenges of the future. Still, it will be a challenging process that will ultimately require the combination of creative, problem-focused leadership with skilled diplomatic deal-brokering among the allies. It is a challenge worth taking up, however, for the member states as well as for the broader transatlantic relationship.

APPENDIX

Summary Tables

Table A.1
Central Threats and Problems, Compared by Perception

Problem Area	United States	United Kingdom	Western Europe	Eastern Europe
Afghanistan	5	5	4	2
Pakistan	5	5	3	1
Iran nuclear-missile threat	5	5	5	4
Al Qaeda	5	5	4	4
Deterring China in the straits	5	3	2	1
Failed states	3	3	4	3
Deterrence against Russia	3	4	3	5
Middle East security	4	4	4	2
WMD proliferation	4	4	4	4
Cyberthreats	3	3	3	3

NOTE: The judgments in this table are subjective and intended for heuristic purposes. They are made on a scale of 0 to 5, with 0 being low and 5 being high; all are significant.

Table A.2
Main Implications of Each Direction

Direction	Strategy	Illustrative Hard Strategy and Requirements	Illustrative Soft Strategy and Requirements	Partnership Requirements	Political Factors
Refocus on Europe	Détente and deterrence	Maintain strategic deterrence Reinforce conventional deterrent Stabilization on European periphery	New effort on NATO-Russia Council Temporarily freeze enlargement	No partnerships	Least demanding politically
Focus on nonstate threats	Hybrid	Special operations forces Small-scale power projection Cyberdefense and counterforce Develop NATO's own capabilities	Coordination with police Intelligence sharing	Cooperative, but not membership-oriented Information sharing Operations basing Border security and monitoring	Relative high political feasibility Potential issues over strategy
Focus on the greater Middle East	Partnerships and deterrence	Retain power for conventional intervention	Develop partnerships Conduct SSR and SFA Confidence building	Cooperative, could be membership-oriented Develop partner defense sector Prepare partners for regional peacekeeping operations Prepare partners for joint peacekeeping operations with NATO Gain access to partner resources for regional operations	Politically challenging Highly beneficial to U.S. interests
Focus on fragile states	Prevention and intervention	Small- to medium-scale intervention capability Stabilization operations COIN	Conduct SSR and SFA Establish NATO lessons-learned process for SSR Establish NATO early-warning prevention measures Prepare humanitarian and disaster response	Cooperative, but not necessarily membership-oriented Involve partners in NATO structures, without Article V commitment	Relationship with EU and UN Geographical scope could raise issues

Table A.2—Continued

Direction	Strategy	Illustrative Hard Strategy and Requirements	Illustrative Soft Strategy and Requirements	Partnership Requirements	Political Factors
Global alliance of liberal democracies	Various, political and military	Depends on suboption chosen Potentially, major combat operations Intervention and power projection Deterrence Extensive development of NATO commands	Reform of NATO internal decisionmaking structures	Membership-oriented Global Platforms for global operations Contributions to global operations Interoperability focus	Very significant political challenges

Bibliography

Allin, Dana H., Gilles Andréani, Philippe Errera, and Gary Samore, *Repairing the Damage: Possibilities and Limits of Transatlantic Consensus*, Abingdon, UK : Routledge for the International Institute of Strategic Studies, Adelphi Paper 389, August 2007.

Asmus, Ronald D., Richard L. Kugler, and F. Stephen Larrabee, "What Will NATO Enlargement Cost," *Survival*, Vol. 38, No. 3, Autumn 1996, pp. 5–26. As of September 1, 2009:
http://www.rand.org/pubs/reprints/RP622/

Atlantic Council, *Saving Afghanistan: An Appeal and Plan for Urgent Action*, issue brief, Washington, D.C., January 28, 2008. As of September 1, 2009:
http://www.acus.org/publication/saving-afghanistan-appeal-and-plan-urgent-action

Bertelsmann Foundation, *Trans-Atlantic Briefing Book: Managing Expectations, Expanding the Partnership, Shaping the Agenda for 2009*, Washington, D.C., November 6, 2008. As of September 1, 2009:
http://www.bertelsmann-stiftung.de/bst/en/media/xcms_bst_dms_26669_26670_2.pdf

Bet-El, Illana, and Rupert Smith, "The Bell Tolls for NATO," *National Interest*, January–February 2008.

Brzezinski, Zbigniew, "An Agenda for NATO," *Foreign Affairs*, Vol. 88, No. 5, September–October 2009, pp. 2–20.

Capezza, David, "Rethinking NATO's Strategic Concept," *New Atlanticist: Policy and Analysis Blog*, Washington, D.C., December 22, 2008. As of July 14, 2009:
http://www.acus.org/new_atlanticist/rethinking-natos-strategic-concept

Daalder, Ivo, and James Goldgeier, "Global NATO," *Foreign Affairs*, September–October 2006.

de Hoop Scheffer, Jaap, secretary general, North Atlantic Treaty Organization, speech, Tel Aviv, Israel, January 11, 2009. As of July 14, 2009:
http://www.nato.int/docu/speech/2009/s090111a.html

———, "Beyond the Bucharest Summit," speech, Brussels Forum in Brussels, Belgium, March 15, 2008. As of July 14, 2009:
http://www.nato.int/docu/speech/2008/s080315a.html

de Nevers, Renée, "NATO's International Security in the Terrorist Era," *International Security*, Vol. 31, No. 4, Spring 2007. As of July 14, 2009:
http://muse.jhu.edu/journals/international_security/v031/31.4denevers.html

Dobbins, James, Seth G. Jones, Keith Crane, Christopher S. Chivvis, Andrew Radin, F. Stephen Larrabee, Nora Bensahel, Brooke Stearns Lawson, and Benjamin W. Goldsmith, *Europe's Role in Nation-Building: From the Balkans to the Congo*, Santa Monica, Calif.: RAND Corporation, MG-722-RC, 2008. As of September 1, 2009:
http://www.rand.org/pubs/monographs/MG722/

Gompert, David C., *French Nuclear Deterrent and Franco-American Cooperation*, Santa Monica, Calif.: RAND Corporation, May 2008. Not available to the general public.

Gompert, David C., and F. Stephen Larrabee, eds., *America and Europe: A Partnership for a New Era*, Cambridge: Cambridge University Press, 1998.

Hamilton, Daniel, Charles Barry, Hans Binnendijk, Stephen Flanagan, Julianne Smith, and James Townsend, *Alliance Reborn: An Atlantic Compact for the 21st Century*, Washington, D.C.: Atlantic Council of the United States; Center for Strategic and International Studies; Center for Technology and National Security Policy, National Defense University; and Center for Transatlantic Relations, Johns Hopkins University, School of Advanced International Studies, February 2009. As of September 1, 2009:
http://www.acus.org/publication/alliance-reborn-atlantic-compact-21st-century

Hendrickson, Ryan C., "The Miscalculation of NATO's Death," *Parameters*, Vol. 37, No. 1, Spring 2007, pp. 98–14. As of July 14, 2009:
http://www.carlisle.army.mil/usawc/parameters/07spring/hendrick.pdf

Kamp, Karl-Heinz, "Toward a New Strategy for NATO," *Survival*, Vol. 51, No. 4, August–September 2009, pp. 21–27.

Katzman, Kenneth, *Afghanistan: Post-War Governance, Security, and U.S. Policy*, Washington, D.C.: Congressional Research Service, RL30588, March 2004.

Kostas, Ifantis, "NATO's Strategic Direction After Riga," *International Journal*, Vol. 62, No. 3, Summer 2007.

Kramer, Franklin D., and Simon Serfaty, *Recasting the Euro-Atlantic Partnership*, Washington, D.C.: Center for Strategic and International Studies, February 1, 2007. As of July 14, 2009:
http://www.csis.org/media/csis/pubs/csis_euroatlantic_feb07.pdf

Kugler, Richard L., *Comparing the RAND and CBO Studies on Costs of NATO Enlargement*, Santa Monica, Calif.: RAND Corporation, July 1996. Not available to the general public.

Larrabee, F. Stephen, *NATO's Eastern Agenda in a New Strategic Era*, Santa Monica, Calif.: RAND Corporation, MR-1744-AF, 2003. As of September 1, 2009:
http://www.rand.org/pubs/monograph_reports/MR1744/

Larrabee, F. Stephen, Jerrold D. Green, Ian O. Lesser, and Michele Zanini, *NATO's Mediterranean Initiative: Policy Issues and Dilemmas*, Santa Monica, Calif.: RAND Corporation, MR-957-IMD, 1998. As of September 1, 2009:
http://www.rand.org/pubs/monograph_reports/MR957/

Lesser, Ian O., Jerrold D. Green, F. Stephen Larrabee, and Michele Zanini, *The Future of NATO's Mediterranean Initiative: Evolution and New Steps*, Santa Monica, Calif.: RAND Corporation, MR-1164-SMD, 2000. As of September 1, 2009:
http://www.rand.org/pubs/monograph_reports/MR1164/

Levine, Robert A., and David Ochmanek, *Toward a Stable Transition in Europe: A Conservative/Activist Strategy for the United States*, Santa Monica, Calif.: RAND Corporation, N-3106-AF, August 1990. As of September 1, 2009:
http://www.rand.org/pubs/notes/N3106/

Lindley-French, Julian, "The Capability-Capacity Crunch: NATO's New Capacities for Intervention," *European Security*, Vol. 15, No. 3, September 2006.

Merkel, Angela, and Nicolas Sarkozy, "La sécurité, notre mission commune," *Le Monde*, February 3, 2009. As of July 14, 2009:
http://www.lemonde.fr/opinions/article/2009/02/03/la-securite-notre-mission-commune-par-angela-merkel-et-nicolas-sarkozy_1150337_3232.html

Molander, Roger C., Stuart E. Johnson, Caroline Reilly, and Camille A. Sawak, *Nuclear Strategy and Policy Revisited: An Analytic Framework for the Next NPR and QDR*, Santa Monica, Calif.: RAND Corporation, April 2009. Not available to the general public.

Morelli, Vincent, and Paul Gallis, *NATO in Afghanistan: A Test of Transatlantic Alliance*, Washington, D.C.: Congressional Research Service, RL33627, January 7, 2008.

NATO—*see* North Atlantic Treaty Organization.

"NATO Chief Calls for New 'Strategic Concept'—Europe—*International Herald Tribune*," *New York Times*, February 11, 2007. As of September 1, 2009:
http://www.nytimes.com/2007/02/11/world/europe/11iht-nato.4554978.html

Naumann, Klaus, John Shalikashvili, The Lord Inge, Jacques Lanxade, and Henk van den Breemen, with Benjamin Bilski and Douglas Murray, *Towards a Grand Strategy for an Uncertain World: Renewing Transatlantic Partnership*, Lunteren, Netherlands: Noaber Foundation, 2007. As of July 14, 2009: http://www.csis.org/media/csis/events/080110_grand_strategy.pdf

Necas, Pavel, *Beyond Tradition: New Alliance's Strategic Concept*, Rome: NATO Defense College, Academic Research Branch, 2004.

North Atlantic Treaty Organization, North Atlantic Treaty, Washington, D.C., April 4, 1949. As of September 2, 2009:
http://www.nato.int/docu/basictxt/treaty.htm

———, *The Alliance's Strategic Concept*, April 24, 1999. As of September 1, 2009:
http://www.nato.int/cps/en/natolive/official_texts_27433.htm?selectedLocale=en

———, "The Future Tasks of the Alliance: Report of the Council," ministerial communiqué, Brussels, December 13–14, 1967, updated October 23, 2000. As of September 1, 2009:
http://www.nato.int/docu/comm/49-95/c671213b.htm

———, *Founding Act on Mutual Relations, Cooperation and Security Between NATO and the Russian Federation*, Paris, May 27, 1997, updated July 12, 2002. As of September 1, 2009:
http://www.nato.int/docu/basictxt/fndact-a.htm

———, "Declaration on Alliance Security," press release, April 4, 2009. As of September 1, 2009:
http://www.nato.int/cps/en/natolive/news_52838.htm?mode=pressrelease

Pursley, David, "NATO's Organizational Evolution: The Case for a Civil Security Committee," *NATO Defense College*, November 2008.

Reiter, Dan, "Why NATO Enlargement Does Not Spread Democracy," *International Security*, Vol. 25, No. 4, Spring 2001. As of July 14, 2009:
http://muse.jhu.edu/journals/international_security/v025/25.4reiter.html

Roi, M. L, and G. Smolynec, "End States, Resource Allocation and NATO Strategy in Afghanistan," *Diplomacy and Statecraft*, Vol. 19, No. 2, June 2008, pp. 289–320.

Ruehle, Michael, "Changing Policy or Staying the Course," *World Security Network*, June 11, 2007. As of July 14, 2009:
http://www.worldsecuritynetwork.com/showArticle3.cfm?article_id=14497

Rynning, Sten, *NATO Renewed: The Power and Purpose of Transatlantic Cooperation*, New York: Palgrave Macmillan, 2005.

Scott, Cameron, *Assessing ISAF: A Baseline Study of NATO's Role in Afghanistan*, London: British American Security Information Council, March 2007. As of September 1, 2009:
http://www.basicint.org/europe/NATO/afghanistan.pdf

Sherwood-Randall, Elizabeth, *Alliances and American National Security*, Strategic Studies Institute, U.S. Army War College, October 2006. As of July 14, 2009:
http://www.strategicstudiesinstitute.army.mil/pdffiles/PUB730.pdf

———, "Is NATO Dead or Alive?" *Huffington Post*, April 1, 2008. As of July 14, 2009:
http://www.huffingtonpost.com/elizabeth-sherwoodrandall/is-nato-dead-or alive_b_94469.html

Sky, Emma, "Increasing ISAF's Impact on Stability on Afghanistan," *Defense and Security Analysis*, Vol. 23, No. 1, March 2007.

Struck, Peter, Federal Minister of Defence, "Future of NATO," speech, 40th Munich Conference on Security Policy, February 7, 2004. As of July 14, 2009:
http://www.europarl.europa.eu/meetdocs/committees/afet/20040217NATO/Struck.pdf

Suhrke, Astri, "A Contradictory Mission? NATO from Stabilization to Combat in Afghanistan," *International Peacekeeping*, Vol. 15, No. 2, April 2008, pp. 214–236. As of July 14, 2009:
http://www.cmi.no/publications/file/?3038=a-contradictory-mission

Thomson, James, "U.S. Interests and the Fate of the Alliance," *Survival*, Vol. 45, No. 4, Winter 2003–2004, pp. 207–220.

U.S. General Accounting Office, *NATO, U.S. Assistance to the Partnership for Peace*, Washington, D.C., GAO-01-734, July 2001. As of September 1, 2009:
http://purl.access.gpo.gov/GPO/LPS15511

Van Ham, Peter, "NATO and the Madonna Curve: Why a New Strategic Concept Is Vital," *NATO Review*, March 2008. As of September 1, 2009:
http://www.nato.int/docu/review/2008/03/ART5/EN/

Van Heuven, Marten, *Where Will NATO Be Ten Years from Now?* Bonn: Zentrum für Europäuscge Integrationsforschung Rheinische Friedrich-Wilhelms-Universität Bonn, 2000.

Volker, Kurt, U.S. Permanent Representative on the North Atlantic Council, "Building a Stronger Transatlantic Community, and a Modern NATO," speech, German Marshall Fund, Brussels, Belgium, September 29, 2008. As of July 14, 2009:
http://nato.usmission.gov/ambassador/2008/Amb_Volker_092908.htm

Williams, Ellen, "Out of Area and Very Much in Business? NATO, the U.S., and the Post-9/11 International Security Environment," *Comparative Strategy*, Vol. 27, No. 1, 2008, pp. 65–78.

Wilson, Peter A., Lowell Schwartz, and Howard J. Shatz, "Eurasian Invasion," *National Interest*, May–June 2008.